BODY NEEDS

Carbohydrates
for a Healthy Body

Hazel King

Heinemann Library
Chicago, Illinois

Library of Congress Cataloging-in-Publication Data
King, Hazel.
  Carbohydrates for a healthy body / Hazel King.
    p. cm. -- (Body needs)
  Summary: Describes what carbohydrates are, what
types of foods contain them, how they are digested and
used to produce energy, and their role in a healthy diet.
  Includes bibliographical references and index.
  ISBN 978 1 432921 86 6 (hb)
  ISBN 978 1 432921 92 7 (pb)
  1. Carbohydrates in the body--Juvenile literature.
[1. Carbohydrates. 2. Nutrition.]   I. Title. II. Series.
  QP701.K565 2003
  612.3'96--dc21

                                    2002012642

j 612.3
  KiN   OCLC   3/11/11 Gift

The author would like to thank Thomas King and Frank
Reakes for their stories.

We would like to thank Dr. Sarah Schenker and Nicole A.
Clark for their invaluable assistance in the preparation
of this book.

Every effort has been made to contact copyright holders
of any material reproduced in this book. Any omissions
will be rectified in subsequent printings if notice is given
to the publishers.

Disclaimer
All the Internet addresses (URLs) given in this book were
valid at the time of going to press. However, due to the
dynamic nature of the Internet, some addresses may
have changed, or sites may have ceased to exist since
publication. While the author and publishers regret any
inconvenience this may cause readers, no responsibility
for any such changes can be accepted by either the
author or the publishers.

Acknowledgments
We would like to thank the following for allowing their
pictures to be reproduced in this publication: ©Action
plus: p. **33**; ©Gareth Boden: pp. **8**, **11**, **12**, **17**, **21**, **23**, **34**,
35, **42**; ©Getty/FPG: p. **40**; ©Gettyone Stone: p. **24**; ©Liz
Eddison: pp. **6**, **7**, **9**, **13**, **20**, **28**, **38**, **43**; ©Photolibrary
Group Ltd: pp. **29** (Foodpix/Kurt Wilson), **30** (Foodpix/
Brian Hagiwara), **31** (Fresh Food Images/Hilary Moore),
37 (Corbis); ©Robert Harrison: p. **4**; ©SPL/Quest: p.
16; ©Trevor Clifford: p. **36**; ©Tudor Photography: p. **5**;
©USDA Center for Nutrition Policy and Promotion p. **41**;
©Zefa: p. **39**.

Contents

Any words appearing in the text in bold, **like this**, are explained in the glossary.

Why Do We Need to Eat?

Eating can be a lot of fun, especially midnight snacks or special treats, but have you ever stopped to wonder why we eat? Food is not there just for our pleasure—it is also needed to keep us alive and healthy.

Nutrients

All foods and drinks provide **energy** and **nutrients**. The main nutrients are carbohydrates, **fats,** and **proteins**. Nutrients are needed to provide energy and help your body grow and repair itself. This book is about carbohydrates, what they are, and how the body uses them. You will need to find out about the other nutrients that your body needs to be healthy. Most foods provide a mixture of different types of nutrients, but some provide more of one type of nutrient than another. Your body needs nutrients every day—this is why you have to eat food. In addition, you must drink water, which, although not a nutrient, is essential for health.

Important roles

Each nutrient has an important job to do in the body. For example, you may know that carbohydrates provide the body with energy. Carbohydrates are provided by foods like bread, pasta, rice, sugar, and potatoes. Fats also provide energy. Foods like butter, oil, or margarine contain fats, and a small amount of them can provide a lot of energy. Protein is provided by foods like meat, fish, eggs, nuts, and beans. Protein is needed to help make new **cells** throughout the body.

» Without the energy that food provides, leading a healthy, active life would not be possible.

This diagram explains the different nutrients and their role in the body. Only some of the **vitamins** and **minerals** your body needs are shown.

CARBOHYDRATES provide your body with the energy it needs physically (to move around) and internally (breathing, heart beating, brain working).

B VITAMINS help to release energy from food.

VITAMIN A helps eyesight and growth of the skin.

WATER makes up a large proportion of the body. It transports substances and allows **chemical reactions** to take place in the body.

CALCIUM helps to make strong bones and teeth.

VITAMIN E helps keep the body healthy.

VITAMIN C helps to keep skin and gums healthy.

FATS provide energy and vitamins A, D, E, and K, help keep us warm, and supply energy if it is not supplied by carbohydrates.

VITAMIN D works with calcium to build strong bones and teeth.

IRON is important for giving blood cells their red color.

PROTEIN is needed to make new cells and repair any damaged ones. Protein is the main substance found in muscles, skin, and internal **organs**.

What Are Carbohydrates?

There are three types of carbohydrate found in the diet: sugar, starch, and **fiber**.

Sugars

Sugars are sometimes called simple carbohydrates because they are made up of small numbers of **molecules**. A molecule is a very small part of a substance. Molecules of sugar are very small, so they are absorbed into our bloodstream very easily when we eat foods that contain sugar. Sugars can be found in foods such as fruits, honey, and even milk. These foods contain **natural sugars**. Sugars also come in a variety of forms, such as granulated sugar, powdered sugar, and brown sugar. These are added to other foods—for example, to cookies. All types of sugar provide your body with energy.

Starches

Starches are more complicated than sugars, so they take longer for your body to **digest**. During digestion all foods are broken down into molecules. When starches are broken down, they end up as molecules of **glucose**. Glucose is a sugar. This means that starches are actually made up of lots of glucose molecules joined together, so they also provide your body with energy. Foods containing starches include potatoes, rice, pasta, bread, couscous, and polenta.

Carbohydrates can be found in a wide variety of foods.

Fiber

Fiber is the most complicated carbohydrate. Unlike sugar and starch, fiber does not provide you with energy, but it does have an important role to play during the digestion of food. Foods that provide lots of fiber include any **whole wheat** products, such as bread, brown rice, pasta, and some breakfast cereals. All fruits and vegetables, pulses (peas, beans, and lentils), oats, barley, and nuts will provide some fiber.

CHOOSING FOOD

Today, most people can choose from a wide variety of foods. Lots of different foods are available, including ready-made meals and takeout food.

What is the carbohydrate in my food?

Food	Source of carbohydrate
pizza	pizza base
chicken and rice	rice and any vegetables
lasagna	pasta
grilled cheese	bread
lemonade/cola	sugar

All the foods in this meal of pasta and vegetables, garlic bread, milk, and fruit contain carbohydrates.

Sugars and Starches

Sugars

Many people say they have a "sweet tooth" because they enjoy the taste of sweet foods. Foods have been sweetened for centuries. Honey was used by the ancient Romans to add sweetness and to make drinks such as **mead**. Today, there is a huge range of different sugars available to use in food preparation.

golden syrup

superfine sugar

granulated sugar

maple syrup

sugar cubes

powdered sugar

brown sugar

honey

sugar crystals

dark brown sugar

 Sugar comes in many different forms.

The role of sugars

Sugars can be very useful when preparing foods. Sugars are sweet, so they are often added to savory foods, such as tomato sauce, to make them more appealing. Sugars can be used to add color to foods, either by using brown sugar or because when sugars are cooked they turn a golden-brown color. Sugars are used to **preserve** some foods, such as jam, and are used to make food look attractive when used as icing or decoration.

Starches

Starches are used very differently from sugars in the preparation of food. First of all, starches are not sweet. In fact, on its own a starch is quite bland—imagine eating raw flour! Most starchy foods have other ingredients added to them when meals are made. For example, pasta is served with a sauce, baked potatoes have a filling added, and bread is made into sandwiches or toast.

Starches are still very useful when preparing food. Starches are able to thicken liquids. If potatoes are added to casseroles, the sauce will become less runny. Cornstarch is another example of a starch being used to thicken foods. It can be used to thicken liquids or sauces and is also added to custard powder to help make custard.

Starches absorb (take in) liquids, so when rice or potatoes are cooked in a saucepan of water, they become soft because of the water they absorb.

Starch facts

When starchy foods are eaten, they are broken down into simple sugars (glucose). If you chew a piece of bread for a few minutes, you will find it eventually tastes sweet. This is because the starch is being broken down by the saliva in your mouth.

>> These starch-rich potatoes are being cooked in a saucepan by simmering them in water. The hard, raw potatoes absorb water during cooking and become soft.

Complicated Fiber

Fiber is often referred to as a **complex carbohydrate** because it has a complicated structure. The human **digestive system** is unable to break it down, so the body does not get any nutrients from fiber. But the fiber is important because it helps the body's digestion. Fiber helps to make waste products soft and easy to pass out of the body. You will find out more about the digestive system on pages 14 and 15.

Insoluble fiber

There are two types of fiber: **insoluble fiber** and **soluble fiber**. The first is found in **bran** and products containing bran. Foods like whole wheat bread are made from wheat, which contains bran. It is known as insoluble fiber because it cannot **dissolve** in a liquid such as water.

Whole wheat products are sometimes called unrefined foods. Wheat can be **processed** so that most of the outer bran is removed and the flour that is produced is white in color. This type of flour provides some fiber. But if all the wheat grain is used (including the bran and **germ**), the flour that results contains a lot more fiber, which is helpful for your digestive system. Products made with this type of flour are less "refined." Insoluble fiber passes through the body without changing very much at all. It can soak up liquids inside your body and helps food move through your digestive system easily.

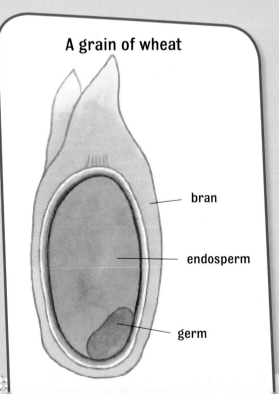

A grain of wheat

bran

endosperm

germ

FIBER AND COOKING

When using ingredients that contain fiber, you have to remember that they will act a bit differently. For example, if you make bread or pastries using whole wheat flour, you must add extra liquid because the bran will soak up more liquid than white flour. Foods made with whole wheat flour will also tend to become dry more quickly than products made using white flour.

Oats are a good source of soluble fiber, so eating oatmeal for breakfast is a great start to the day!

Soluble fiber

Soluble fiber is found in foods like oats, vegetables, and fruits. By including plenty of fruits and vegetables in your diet, you keep your digestive system healthy. You will also benefit from the various vitamins and minerals that the fruits and vegetables provide.

Soluble fiber can help lower blood **cholesterol** levels. Soluble fiber in the diet can bind to bile **acids**, which are released into the digestive tract (see pages 14 and 15) to aid the digestion of fat in the diet. The binding of bile acids to soluble fiber means that they are not able to be reabsorbed by the body to be used again. This means the body needs to make more bile acids, and this process uses up cholesterol, helping to lower levels in the blood.

Energy Efficient

You need energy

Carbohydrates are an excellent source of energy. Energy is needed so that your body can grow, repair itself, and keep warm. Even when you are asleep, your body needs energy in order to function properly. Without energy you would not survive. You need it to breathe, digest food, and even think! In fact, your brain is the most energy-demanding organ in your body.

Every cell in your body needs the sugar called glucose, and it is particularly important to your **nervous system**, red blood cells, and brain. Glucose is the sugar that carbohydrates are broken down into when they are digested. After eating foods containing carbohydrates, some of the energy will be used right away, while the rest of it will be stored.

Glycogen stores

Any glucose that is not immediately needed by the body is stored in the **liver** or stays in the muscles. However, it is not stored as glucose. Instead it is converted into a substance known as **glycogen**. Carbohydrates are a great source of energy because glycogen is quickly and easily turned back into glucose as soon as it is needed.

Measuring energy

The energy that is released from food is measured in **calories** or **kilojoules**. People can look at food labels to see how much energy will be provided by a meal or product.

 The human body uses 60 calories every hour just to sleep!

Energy from food

All foods and most drinks provide energy. Water is one drink that does not supply any calories. The amount of energy supplied by a food depends on what the food contains. Foods that are high in fats will have a high energy value because fat provides the most calories.

There are typically 4 calories per gram of carbohydrate. For example, a slice of bread has 15 grams of carbohydrates, which makes 60 calories from carbohydrates (15 grams x 4 calories = 60 calories). Fat has 9 calories per gram, and protein 4 calories per gram.

CARBOHYDRATES AND FATS

It is interesting to compare the number of calories that carbohydrate foods supply on their own and when combined with fats. For example, 100 grams (3.5 ounces) of boiled potatoes provide 110 calories. But when potatoes are made into French fries (which means they are fried in oil), the energy values rise dramatically to 310 calories.

 All foods provide energy, but different foods supply energy in different amounts of calories. Butter is higher in energy value than meat or bagels.

Digesting Carbohydrates

Carbohydrates may be a good source of energy, but until they have been broken down, your body cannot use the energy. The process of breaking down food is called digestion. After food has been digested, it must be absorbed in a form that can be used by your body.

Chew it

The first stage of digestion takes place in your mouth. You physically start breaking down the food with your teeth by biting and chewing it. At the same time chemicals called **enzymes** in your saliva start attacking the starch. Enzymes are chemicals that speed up the breakdown of food. Large molecules in food are broken down into smaller ones. The saliva also makes the food moist and easier to swallow.

Swallow it

The moist, chewed-up food is then swallowed and passes down a long tube called the **esophagus** (see diagram). At the end of the esophagus is the stomach, which is like a stretchy bag. Carbohydrate foods stay in the stomach for about two to three hours while being churned around and made into a mushy liquid called **chyme**. **Digestive juices** containing enzymes continue to attack the food and break it down.

Absorb it

The chyme gradually passes from the stomach into the **small intestine**, where further breakdown takes place. By now the food consists of tiny molecules, which are small enough to pass through the walls of the small intestine into the bloodstream (see diagram). You will find out more about absorption on pages 16 and 17.

Move it

You will see from the diagram that the digestive system is very long. Food cannot pass along it by itself—it needs some help. This help comes from the muscles in the walls of the intestines, which squeeze and relax, pushing the food along.

Release it

Any food that is not useful to the body will not be absorbed into the blood. Instead it will pass from the small intestine into the **large intestine**. This is where any insoluble fiber will end up. As the remaining food particles (small pieces) travel along the large intestine, water is absorbed back into the body. Finally, waste matter is released from the body through the anus when you go to the bathroom.

Food facts

Food can take at least 24 hours to travel through the intestines. When the intestines are stretched out, they are about as long as a school bus!

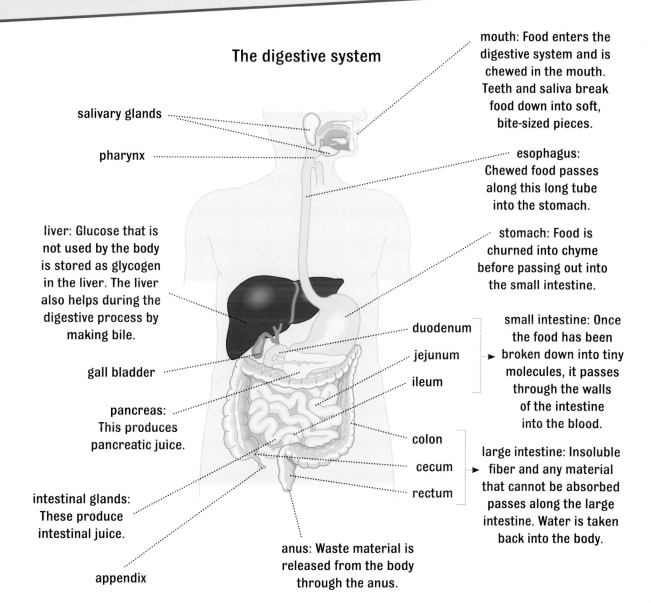

The digestive system

salivary glands

pharynx

liver: Glucose that is not used by the body is stored as glycogen in the liver. The liver also helps during the digestive process by making bile.

gall bladder

pancreas: This produces pancreatic juice.

intestinal glands: These produce intestinal juice.

appendix

mouth: Food enters the digestive system and is chewed in the mouth. Teeth and saliva break food down into soft, bite-sized pieces.

esophagus: Chewed food passes along this long tube into the stomach.

stomach: Food is churned into chyme before passing out into the small intestine.

duodenum

jejunum

ileum

small intestine: Once the food has been broken down into tiny molecules, it passes through the walls of the intestine into the blood.

colon

cecum

rectum

large intestine: Insoluble fiber and any material that cannot be absorbed passes along the large intestine. Water is taken back into the body.

anus: Waste material is released from the body through the anus.

Absorbing Carbohydrates

The nutrients in the food that you eat need to get to all the cells in your body. There would be no point eating and digesting food unless your body had some way of getting the food into your bloodstream and transporting it around the body. The process that your body uses to do this is called absorption. This takes place in the small intestine.

Small intestine

By the time you are fully grown, your small intestine is about 7 meters (23 feet) long. It is made up of three parts: the **duodenum**, the **jejunum**, and the **ileum**. Carbohydrates and proteins are absorbed in the jejunum, but fats are absorbed in the ileum. The small intestine looks like a folded tube that joins your stomach and your large intestine.

Tiny villi

The inside lining of the small intestine is covered with millions of tiny hair-like projections called **villi**. Each villus is about half a millimeter long and has even smaller "microvilli" covering it! This is a very clever way to increase the surface area of the small intestine. Surface area is the space occupied by the surface of something.

Molecules of digested food pass through the walls of the villi and into the blood vessels. It is important that all the food molecules are absorbed into your bloodstream so you can benefit from the nutrients. To do this, there must be as much surface area as possible to allow all the molecules to pass through the cell walls.

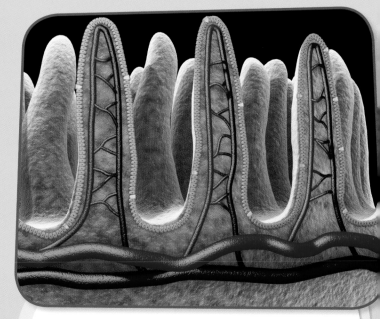

 The lining of the small intestine is covered with villi, and the villi are covered with microvilli. Here you can see microvilli from the small intestine.

Molecules of food

When carbohydrate foods are broken down, the tiny glucose molecules are absorbed through the walls of the small intestine and into the blood. The blood transports the molecules to the liver for processing. The food molecules include glucose from the breakdown of carbohydrates, **amino acids** from the breakdown of protein, and **fatty acids** from the breakdown of fats.

Leftover matter

Any food that remains after the absorption process has to be removed from the body. This sludgy matter contains the fiber that helps to keep the waste soft and bulky. This means it can leave the body more easily.

Body fact

It may be surprising to learn that much of your body is made up of water. There is water in your blood, saliva, urine, and all the cells of your body, including your bones, muscles, and skin. As you can lose as much as 3 liters (6.3 pints) of water every day in your sweat, urine, and breath, it is important to replace that moisture.

Your body gets water from the foods you eat and liquids you drink. Without water, the body would not be able to absorb nutrients from food.

Energy Release

Food for fuel

Your body needs fuel to provide you with energy in the same way a car needs gasoline to make it go. Carbohydrate foods are the best type of "fuel" for your body because they are broken down into glucose, which can be used by every cell in your body.

Your bloodstream is a bit like a car's gas tank. It needs to have a constant level of glucose in the blood so that cells can use it whenever energy is needed. If there is more than your body needs, the liver changes the extra glucose into glycogen and stores it. The liver also changes the glycogen back into glucose as soon as the glucose energy in the blood is used up.

Turning food into fuel

The process of turning food into energy is a complicated one. Every cell in your body has a tiny "energy factory" where a series of chemical reactions happen. The result is the release of energy. **Oxygen** is needed for this to happen properly. During this process **carbon dioxide** and water are produced. There is carbon dioxide in our breath when we breathe out. The amount of energy you need depends on your weight, age, whether you are a boy or a girl, and the type and amount of activity you are doing. Children and teenagers require a lot of energy compared to their size because their bodies are still growing. Boys tend to need more energy than girls, and girls tend to have more body fat than boys. Different activities need different amounts of energy; running requires more energy than walking, but walking requires more than sitting. The weather can also affect your energy levels. If the weather is cold your body will have to work hard trying to keep you warm.

Be active!

People who are inactive are more prone to weight gain than those who lead active lifestyles. It is recommended that children and young people aim to do at least an hour of physical activity every day, and that adults aim to do at least 30 minutes of physical activity five days a week.

Constant levels

The best foods for keeping your **blood sugar levels** constant are those that contain complex carbohydrates. This is because they are gradually broken down and release their sugar slowly into the bloodstream. Whole wheat foods, beans, fruits, and some vegetables are all slow-release carbohydrate foods. Sweets, on the other hand, cause blood sugar levels to rise quickly. This in turn makes the body try to lower the level. Blood sugar levels fall again, creating a feeling of hunger. If more sweets are eaten, the whole process starts again.

 This diagram shows how energy is released from food when we eat.

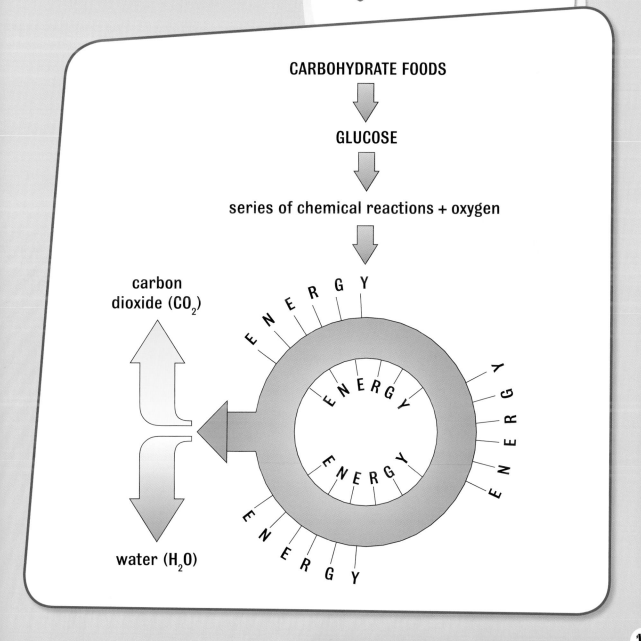

CARBOHYDRATE FOODS

GLUCOSE

series of chemical reactions + oxygen

carbon dioxide (CO_2)

water (H_2O)

ENERGY

Energy and Exercise

The amount of energy you need just to maintain your body, while you are doing absolutely nothing, is known as the **basal metabolic rate** (**BMR**). The rate depends on the amount of muscle in the body. This means it will vary according to your weight, age, and whether you are a boy or a girl. Boys usually require more kilojoules than girls per day and the difference increases as children get older.

In and out

The energy your body receives from food is known as its energy input. The amount of energy it uses is its output. Ideally, the input and output should be roughly the same. However, if your energy input is higher than your output, your body will store any extra as fat and you may gain weight. On the other hand, if your input is lower than your output, you may lose weight. A good diet is one that ensures you stay at a healthy weight.

Nutritionists recommend that most of your energy should be provided by carbohydrate foods.

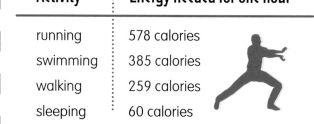

Energy you might need during various activities

Activity	Energy needed for one hour
running	578 calories
swimming	385 calories
walking	259 calories
sleeping	60 calories

Of course, you cannot figure out how much energy you are going to use each day and then eat the right amount of food! Usually people rely on what their body is telling them and eat if they feel hungry and stop when they feel full. However, sometimes it is important to plan ahead, especially if you know you are going to do a lot of exercise. If, for example, you are going to do a lot of running, you would know to fuel your body by eating meals containing pasta a few days beforehand.

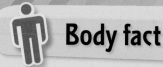

Body fact

When running a **marathon**, your body starts off using blood sugar (glucose) and then it uses glycogen stores. When glycogen runs out, and if no other energy is supplied, the body breaks down fat or protein to make its energy. However, this is much more effort for the body.

TOM'S STORY

Tom King uses plenty of energy doing various sports every week, including baseball, soccer, tennis, and swimming. However, his favorite sport is basketball. He plays forward for his school's team. He knows how to keep up his energy levels and stay healthy. Tom says: "I normally eat things like carrots, cucumbers, and lots of pasta. I have my favorite pasta dishes before a big game and I only have potato chips and soda on special occasions (or when my mom lets me)!"

When you eat pasta, the energy that your body receives from it is released slowly.

Dental Health

Today's healthy-eating advice tells us to reduce the amount of sugar we eat. If you often eat sugary foods, your teeth can become damaged. Sugars left in the mouth attract **bacteria** that multiply, resulting in the production of acid. Acid conditions cause tooth enamel to break down and teeth to become damaged. This is known as tooth decay.

Brush well

After eating sugary foods, your saliva helps the mouth to return to normal — but this takes about 30 minutes. For this reason, if you do eat sweets, it is better to eat them all at once rather than a few at a time. It is also better for your teeth if you choose sweets that can be eaten quickly. Sweets that are sucked give bacteria the conditions they enjoy for longer, so they are likely to cause more damage. Of course, if you can, you should brush your teeth after eating any foods, especially sticky ones. Teeth should be brushed twice a day using a **fluoride** toothpaste.

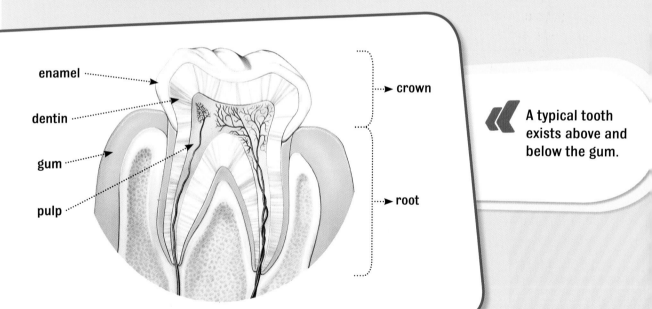

enamel

dentin

gum

pulp

crown

root

A typical tooth exists above and below the gum.

Inside, outside

Sugars can be divided into two categories: those found inside food cells and those that are not. The first type includes glucose, produced when carbohydrates are broken down, and fructose, which is found in some fruits. The second type includes the sugars used during baking (such as granulated sugar and brown sugar) and also honey.

Health experts agree that a healthy diet should include only a small amount of foods containing fructose, the second type of sugar. This is because these sugars are found mainly in foods like cakes, cookies, candies, soda drinks, and many ready-made meals. These foods tend to be high in sugars (as well as fats) and contain few complex carbohydrates.

Sweet treats

Although sugar provides your body with energy, it does not provide any nutrients. Sugar does not contain vitamins, minerals, protein, starches, fiber, or fats. This is another reason why health experts believe it is better to get energy from foods that also provide us with vitamins or other nutrients. When you are hungry, it is better to choose fruit or a sandwich instead of sweets. You will gain more vitamins and minerals, and it will be better for your teeth!

It is fine to eat sweets as a treat every now and then, but always brush your teeth afterward.

Too Much of a Good Thing

Food is the fuel you need to give you energy, but food can also be fun! Other animals do not treat food in the same way that humans do. Animals tend to eat when they are hungry and only eat the food their body needs. People spend much more time thinking about food. They shop for, prepare, cook, and serve food. They can choose to eat at a restaurant or order meals for delivery. Unlike animals, we have a great deal of choice when it comes to food.

 Fast foods may be tasty, but they are often high in fat.

More carbohydrate, less fat

Everyone is being encouraged to include plenty of complex carbohydrate foods in their diet. But the trouble with many of today's meals is that they also include lots of high fat foods. A burger bun, for example, is a good source of starchy carbohydrate, but the burger inside is likely to be very fatty! A whole wheat bread sandwich sounds like a healthy option, but if the bread is very thin and the filling includes lots of cheese and mayonnaise (both of which contain fat), then it is no longer such a healthy choice.

Healthy hearts

"Obesity" is a term that is often used today. It refers to when a person is very overweight. Obesity is one of the causes of **coronary heart disease**. It also affects what type of activity a person is able to do.

The type of foods on offer today is part of the reason why there has been an increase in obesity and coronary heart disease. A lot of "fast food" is high in fats and sugars and contains few complex carbohydrates. Food such as hamburgers and hot dogs only fill you up for a short time, so you feel hungry and need to eat again fairly soon.

Lack of exercise

Beyond eating high fat meals, people do not exercise as much as they used to. Fewer young people walk to school because many households have a car, and they spend more of their leisure time doing activities that do not require much energy, such as playing computer games. In addition to eating a healthy diet it is important to take care of your body by getting regular exercise and plenty of fresh air.

Many people are overweight because they eat too many calories. The high fat content of many meals contributes to this because fat is higher in calories than protein and carbohydrates. Fat is also easily transferred into the fat cells compared with the other nutrients that have to break down first.

Staying Healthy

You have read a lot so far about the importance of the energy supplied by starchy carbohydrate foods. However, they have many other health benefits, too. Complex carbohydrates, such as those in whole grain foods, beans, vegetables, and fruits, can help reduce the risk of problems with the digestive system. This is because foods containing fiber help waste products travel through the digestive system (see pages 14 and 15). If there are no complex carbohydrates in the diet, the waste is not able to absorb moisture and becomes hard and dry. This makes it much more difficult for the waste to leave the body, leading to problems such as constipation.

Toilet trouble

Constipation is when someone has trouble going to the bathroom. The waste matter (known as feces or stool) is hard and does not travel easily through the digestive system. Sometimes this causes straining while on the toilet, which can then lead to **hemorrhoids**. Another condition that can affect the digestive system is diverticular disease. This happens when pockets appear in the lining of the large intestine (also known as the colon), into which waste material gets trapped. Eating complex carbohydrates may also help reduce the risk of getting bowel cancer later in life.

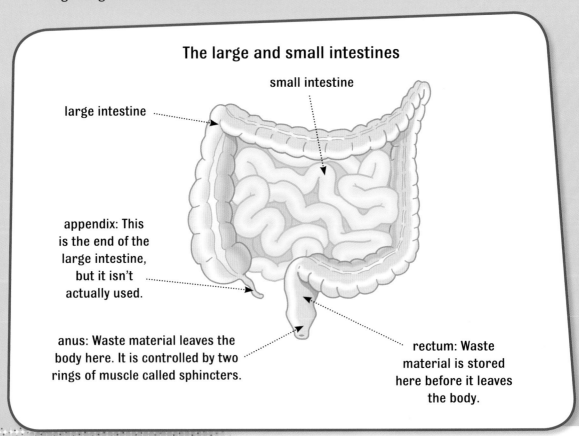

The large and small intestines

small intestine

large intestine

appendix: This is the end of the large intestine, but it isn't actually used.

anus: Waste material leaves the body here. It is controlled by two rings of muscle called sphincters.

rectum: Waste material is stored here before it leaves the body.

 Eating a balanced diet is the best way to stay healthy.

Healthy carbohydrates

Following a diet that contains plenty of "healthy" carbohydrates can also help reduce the chance of having appendicitis, which is what happens when the appendix becomes inflamed. Again, this is because waste material that is too dry becomes trapped in the appendix.

Not eating enough

Not eating enough food for a long time can be as harmful as eating too much. Your body needs a healthy, balanced diet so that you can grow, repair your body, and do all the activities you want to do. Some people in **developing countries** do not always get enough food and may suffer from diseases due to a lack of nutrients. Even in the Western world, where there should be enough food for everyone, people sometimes suffer because they are not eating the right things. If people do not have much money, they may buy cheap foods that are filling, such as French fries, and eat these every day. Fries provide energy in the form of carbohydrates and fats, but they do not provide many of the other nutrients. If people eat a diet low in nutrients for a long time, they will become sick and their bodies will not grow properly.

Labeling Sugar

Today, people are being encouraged to try to reduce the amount of sugar they eat. This includes the sugar that is added to drinks or used in food preparation. The natural sugars found in fruits and some vegetables are not seen as a health problem.

It contains what?

Many of today's ready-made meals and processed foods have to have extra ingredients added to them. It would not be possible to follow a cookbook recipe for apple pie and then expect it to stay fresh in the stores for a week. Products such as chocolate ice cream bars would not work unless extra ingredients were added. Sometimes **additives** called preservatives are used to make foods last longer. Additives called stabilizers stop ingredients from separating out.

Food fact

The ingredients listed below are from a chocolate ice cream bar containing caramel and nuts. They show that both sugar and glucose syrup are present in the caramel and in the ice cream.

You may be surprised by the foods that have sugar added.

Ingredients: Concentrated skimmed milk, milk chocolate (25%), caramel (8%) (concentrated skimmed milk, glucose syrup, sugar, vegetable fat, butteroil, stabilizer (E410), sugar, glucose syrup, vegetable fat, whey solids, wheat crispies, (1%) (wheat flour, salt, raising agent E503), peanuts (1%) stabilizers, emulsifier, flavoring, color.

INGREDIENTS:
Tomatoes (126g per 100g Ketchup)
Spirit Vinegar, Glucose Syrup, Sugar
Salt, Spice and Herb Extracts. Spice
Garlic Powder
SUITABLE FOR A GLUTEN FREE DIET
2mg Lycopene per 10ml serving

Sugars are often added to food products, particularly those that have reduced fat. Sugar can help to make foods tasty and give foods "body." However, it is not always possible to tell how much sugar is in a product just by reading the ingredients list.

All food products must be labeled to show their ingredients. Sugars are often listed under their chemical names rather than just saying "sugar." For example, the following are all names of sugars: sucrose, glucose, lactose, fructose, invert sugar, syrup, molasses, honey, and glucose syrup. This is why consumers do not always know exactly what they are eating or just how much sugar is contained in a product.

Sweet enough?

Many foods have added sweetness without the addition of sugar. Artificial sweeteners have been around for many years, and they have the advantage of adding sweetness without adding energy (calories). Non-sugar sweeteners are particularly useful for people with **diabetes**, who must be careful about the amount of sugar in their diet.

Many people use artificial sweeteners to avoid the calories in sugar or because they have to limit the sugar in their diet.

Food Labels

The way food products are labeled, and the information put on the label, is carefully controlled by law. It is important that people are not misled by a food label, particularly someone who has an **allergy** to an ingredient. You will find out more about food allergies on page 34.

Food products must, by law, show the following information:

- a name
- a list of ingredients, starting with the heaviest and ending with the lightest
- a label to show shelf-life, such as "best before" or "use by"
- any special storage conditions or conditions of use
- the manufacturer
- where the food came from
- instructions for use
- weight or volume of the contents (unless it weighs less than 5 grams)
- warnings about possible problems for allergy sufferers.

Packaged food must be accurately labeled so that consumers know exactly what they are buying.

Food fact

"Use by" dates are used for foods that go "bad" quickly and may be unsafe to eat after this date. These dates are found on foods like fresh meat, fish, and cheese.

"Best before" dates are usually found on foods that will keep longer than a few days. They will not be at their best after this date. These dates are found on breakfast cereals, cookies, and canned foods.

What's in a name?

All packaged food must have a name that tells people exactly what is in the package. For example, the label could not say just "flour," because there are lots of different types of flour. It might say "whole wheat self-rising flour" or "all-purpose flour." The label must also say whether the food has been processed. This means that a package of pasta might have a label saying "fresh" or "dried," depending how it has been made.

Reading labels

You can also find different starches listed in ingredients lists. These are starches that have been used in food production. For example, starches such as cornstarch can thicken sauces. Thickeners or thickening agents are often used in reduced-sugar or low-sugar products. Sugar usually makes things set (like jam, for example). When less sugar is used, something else is needed to act as a **gelling agent**. Gelatin and pectin are commonly used as thickeners and may be seen on many food labels.

Starch is needed to thicken food products, such as this sauce being used to top lasagna. Different starches can be seen listed on food labels.

Sugar Control

Glucose is your body's main source of energy. The way your body uses glucose is controlled by several chemicals called **hormones**. One of these hormones is insulin. Unfortunately, some people's bodies are not able to produce enough insulin. This means their bodies cannot control their blood sugar level. The amount of glucose traveling around in their blood can become very high or very low. The result is a disease called diabetes.

Diabetes

A very high or very low level of glucose in the blood is serious. The levels must be controlled. Diabetes can be controlled by either modifying the diet or by taking pills and/or insulin. Some diabetics need a daily injection of insulin, while others only need to be careful about what they eat. A diet high in complex carbohydrates and fiber (including whole wheat bread, whole grain rice and cereals, vegetables, and fruits) is recommended because these foods help to control the rate at which sugar is absorbed into the blood.

Sweet treats

People with diabetes must make sure they do not have too much sugar or sugary foods and drinks, such as candies, cakes, cookies, or soda. Sugary products will cause a sudden rise in blood sugar levels. However, people with diabetes do not have to avoid sweet foods altogether. They can eat sweet treats occasionally, but it is better to eat them after a meal rather than on an empty stomach.

Young and old

It is not clear why people with diabetes do not make enough insulin in their bodies. There are two types of diabetes: type 1 (insulin dependent) and type 2 (non-insulin dependent). The first type usually develops suddenly with severe symptoms and normally happens before the age of 40.

Type 2 diabetes does not require treatment with insulin because some insulin is still produced in the body. This type of diabetes can be controlled by eating healthily or sometimes by pills. This type tends to affect middle-aged and older people, although anyone who is overweight is at a higher risk of developing the disease as they get older.

FRANK'S STORY

Frank Reakes is 13 years old and was diagnosed with diabetes 10 months ago. Frank says: "Before I was diagnosed I noticed something was wrong; in school I couldn't concentrate and frequently asked to go to the bathroom and get water. At home I was never hungry and I especially went to the bathroom at night."

Having diabetes hasn't affected his lifestyle very much because he is still able to enjoy playing sports. However, he now has to avoid desserts and snacks. He also eats lots of complex carbohydrates like rice and pasta.

 Having diabetes can affect the types of food you can eat, but you can still enjoy a wide variety of sports.

Food Allergies

A food allergy is a reaction caused by eating a specific food or foods. Common foods most likely to cause an allergic reaction are milk, eggs, fish, shellfish, nuts, and soybeans. Gluten is found in wheat, which is used to make flour, a carbohydrate food. Celiac disease is the name for an intolerance to gluten.

Gluten

Gluten is a protein found mainly in wheat, although it is also present in rye, barley, and oats. People with celiac disease have a condition in which the walls of their small intestine become damaged if they eat gluten. When the villi (see page 16) in the lining of the small intestine are damaged, nutrients are not absorbed properly. The symptoms include stomach pain, sickness, tiredness, bloating, diarrhea, and loss of weight.

Avoiding foods

Obviously, someone with this allergy must avoid all foods containing gluten. Unfortunately, this includes a huge range of foods, because wheat is used to make flour. Just think how many products are made from flour: cookies, cakes, most breads, pancakes, many sauces, and pastries.

Anyone with celiac disease must avoid foods like these, as they all contain gluten.

Lots of processed foods like desserts, snacks, and ready-made meals include starch-based thickeners containing gluten, so these must be avoided, too. Also, anything containing rye or barley may cause a reaction, as well as foods made using oats, such as oatmeal and pancakes.

Celiac specials

Fortunately, many supermarkets now cater to celiacs and provide a range of gluten-free products. Many foods have gluten-free labels to show they are safe for celiacs to eat. Health food stores have sold products, such as bread and cakes, for celiacs for some time.

Food fact

Someone with celiac disease will need to avoid some or all of the following: barley, bran, cereal filler, malt, modified starch, oats, rusk, rye, semolina, starch, and wheat flour. This means they must read food labels very carefully.

Some foods are labeled "gluten-free."

Staple Starches

A staple food is the main food of a diet and is usually a food that provides energy. Starchy carbohydrate foods are called staple foods because they form a major part of the diet. Different countries and cultures have their own staples, depending on their climate and what they are able to grow. One of the staple foods in the United States is wheat, which grows in many areas throughout the country. The diet of most Americans is based in large part on what can be made with wheat, or the flour made from wheat. Throughout history, bread has been an important filler (food that fills you up) that is fairly cheap for people to buy.

Potatoes

Potatoes are also a staple food that is readily available for Americans. Many "comfort food" dishes use potatoes, such as mashed potatoes, baked potatoes, and French fries. Many people would not consider a meal complete unless it was served with potatoes.

Lots of choice

Today, staple foods do not always have to follow recipes that are native to a particular country. For example, local U.S. bakeries can create breads from around the world. You can choose between ciabatta (from Italy), croissant (from France), naan (from India), and more. This variety makes dining a lot more interesting!

Today, we have a huge variety of breads to choose from.

Pass the pasta

Pasta is traditionally a staple food of Italy. It can now be bought fresh, dry, or as part of a ready-made meal throughout the world. Pasta is made with flour, and sometimes eggs are added. The flour used for making pasta comes from durum wheat. This produces semolina flour, which is fine, gritty, and yellow in color. Once the pasta dough has been made, it is cut, pressed, and molded into different shapes and sizes.

Pasta parties

Pasta is a very healthy food. It is low in fats and high in complex carbohydrates. It even has a "high fiber" version—brown pasta provides more fiber.

Pasta comes in a huge range of shapes, sizes, and colors!

Worldwide Diets

Rice is a staple food of several countries, including India, China, and Japan. Like pasta, rice is low in fat and high in complex carbohydrates. Brown rice contains bran, so it also provides fiber and has slightly more protein, iron, calcium, and B vitamins.

Rice dishes

There are many different varieties of rice, so it is not surprising that there are also many different ways of cooking and serving it. Traditionally, in India, long grain rice is cooked in stock (flavored liquid) with meat, fish, and/or vegetables to make a pilau. Japanese and Chinese dishes tend to use soft, sticky rice that can be shaped with the fingers (as in sushi) or picked up with chopsticks. The Italians are famous for risotto. Ladles of stock are slowly added to the risotto rice until it becomes creamy, plump, and tender.

Food fact

Long grain rice is about four to five times longer than it is wide. Examples include basmati rice and Carolina rice.

Short grain rice has short, plump grains that tend to remain moist and cling together when cooked. Examples include Arborio (risotto) rice and pudding rice.

Cornmeal can be used to make polenta and cornbread.

Gluten free

Rice is also similar to pasta because it is a "slow-release" carbohydrate, so it is a much better source of energy than the "instant" energy provided by sugary foods. In addition, rice is suitable for people with celiac disease because it does not contain any gluten.

Puffed rice

Rice is not only eaten as grain in savory and sweet dishes—it can also be processed to make many other products. Grains of rice can be ground up to turn them into rice flour, ground rice, and flaked rice. These ingredients are then used to make puddings, cakes, cookies, and as thickening agents for soups or stews. Rice can also be "puffed" to make puffed rice cereals and rice cake snacks.

Couscous can be used as an alternative to rice.

Moroccan couscous

"Couscous" is the name of a tiny grain made from finely ground semolina wheat. It cooks very quickly in hot water or by being steamed. Today, you can buy packages of dried couscous, some of which have flavors already added to them. Couscous is also the name of a spicy Moroccan dish that is served on a bed of couscous. Traditionally, couscous was a staple food of North Africa.

Corn or maize?

Corn (also called maize) is a staple food of many countries, including Italy, Mexico, and the United States. It can be used to make a wide range of products, such as tortillas (thin pancakes), polenta (a dough made from maize flour), breakfast cereals, cornbread, and even popcorn!

Eating for Health

It is now known that the diet you eat throughout your life can affect your risk of getting diseases such as coronary heart disease. **Dietary guidelines** have been produced to help people choose a diet that contains foods needed for good health. These guidelines do not tell people *what* to eat, but rather suggest different ways to follow a healthy diet. Dietary guidelines are produced by various health organizations, including governments.

Varied diet

Eating a variety of foods is important. People sometimes end up eating the same foods every day out of habit, laziness, or just because they like them. But in the long term this can lead to a lack of some nutrients and could cause health problems. There is not one single food that contains all the nutrients in the right quantities, which is why everyone should eat a variety of foods. When you think about the thousands of foods available, it must be possible to find different ones that you like to eat.

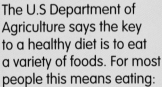

Food fact

The U.S Department of Agriculture says the key to a healthy diet is to eat a variety of foods. For most people this means eating:
- more fruits and vegetables — eat lots! You can choose from fresh, frozen, canned, dried, or juiced.
- more bread, cereals, and potatoes.
- less fat and sugar—try to eat fewer fatty or sugary foods.

 Drinking plenty of water is also part of a healthy diet.

The food pyramid

The "MyPyramid" food pyramid was produced by the U.S. Department of Agriculture's Center for Nutrition Policy and Promotion to help people understand how to eat healthily. It is used by **dieticians**, health professionals, manufacturers, caterers, and in schools. The food pyramid clearly shows the sort of foods that can be included in a healthy diet and in what proportion. For example, the section containing foods providing grains is quite big, while the section showing fats and oils is much smaller. The government website (see page 47) lists the proper servings for your age.

The government website (see page 47) lists the proper servings for your age.

Food fact

Eat five! Did you know that you should aim to eat at least five portions of fruits and vegetables every day?

The food pyramid shows the proportions of different foods that make up a healthy diet.

GRAINS · VEGETABLES · FRUITS · MILK · MEAT & BEANS

Achieving a Balance

Eating a healthy diet is not just about the foods you choose. It is also about the way those foods are prepared and cooked. Potatoes are high in complex carbohydrates and provide vitamin C. But if potatoes are cut into thin slices and deep fried, they will also contain lots of fat. Or, if the potatoes are boiled, left to get cold, and reheated, any vitamin C present is likely to be lost. This is because vitamin C dissolves into the cooking water and is destroyed by heat. So, it is important to consider how foods are cooked.

Thicker fries

Eating a healthy, balanced diet does not mean you have to give up foods you enjoy. It just means you shouldn't eat them all the time. Eating French fries occasionally is fine, and it is even better if you can choose thicker-cut fries. If a potato is cut into thicker pieces rather than thin ones, it will absorb less fat when cooked.

Lots of foods can be just as tasty if they are cooked without using or adding fat. Eggs are a good example. They can be boiled, poached, or scrambled. Bacon is best grilled because the fat can drip into the grill pan, and so you do not have to eat it. Some foods can be "dry fried," which means no extra fat is added to the pan. There are some good nonstick frying pans that make this method possible.

Potatoes can be eaten in a variety of ways. As long as you don't always eat fatty fries, you can enjoy a healthy variety.

Saving vitamins

Vegetables are often cooked by boiling them in water. Some vitamins dissolve into the water during cooking and are lost when the vegetables are drained. It is better to steam or microwave vegetables, as less water is needed and more of the vitamins are saved.

A healthy, balanced diet should be part of everyone's lifestyle.

Carbohydrates in a variety of foods, broken down into starch, sugars, and fiber			
Food	Starches (grams)	Sugars (grams)	Fiber (grams)
1 small banana	2.3	20.9	1.1
1 small can baked beans	24	4	11
100 grams (1 cup) cauliflower	0.2	2.5	1.6
2 slices bread, brown	41.3	4	4
2 slices bread, white	43.8	2	2
100 grams (0.75 cup) flour, wheat, white	76.2	1.5	3.6

Glossary

acid something that tastes sour—for example, vinegar or lemon juice

additive substance (natural or artificial) added to foods to increase their shelf life or to improve their color, flavor, or texture

allergy bad reaction caused by eating a particular food. Some people can become very sick from food allergies.

amino acid building block of proteins. Different amino acids combine together to form a protein.

bacteria microorganisms (living things) that are so small they can only be seen through a microscope. Some are helpful, such as those in our intestines, and some can be harmful, such as those that cause food poisoning.

basal metabolic rate (BMR) rate at which your body burns food when it is completely rested

blood sugar level amount of glucose in the blood. This will rise after sugar has been eaten and will gradually fall until food is eaten again.

bran outer layer of a grain of wheat

calorie measurement of energy supplied by food

carbon dioxide gas present in our breath when we breathe out

cell microscopic living thing that makes up all living matter

chemical reaction something that occurs between two or more chemicals

cholesterol fatty substances found in the body

chyme mushy liquid that passes from the stomach to the small intestine. It is formed from partly digested food mixed with the digestive juices of the stomach.

complex carbohydrate carbohydrate that cannot be broken down by the human digestive system, such as the bran in whole wheat bread

coronary heart disease illness that affects the heart. When the vessels leading to the heart become blocked by fatty substances, the blood cannot get to the heart as easily.

developing country less developed country that is often poor and does not have well established industries and services, such as transportation, schools, or welfare

diabetes when the body does not have enough insulin (a hormone) to control the amount of glucose in the blood

dietary guideline suggestion for healthy eating

dietician person who advises people about what they should eat

digest   process of breaking down food when it is eaten. Digestion starts in the mouth when you bite and chew food and continues until the molecules that make up food are taken into the bloodstream.

digestive juice   liquid containing enzymes that helps to break down food during digestion. Saliva and gastric juices are examples of digestive juices.

digestive system   all the parts of the body that are used to digest food

dissolve   gradually disappear in a liquid

duodenum   first part of the small intestine

energy   what the body needs to stay alive. Energy is supplied by foods.

enzyme   something that helps a chemical reaction to take place faster without being changed itself

esophagus   tube through which food travels from the mouth to the stomach

fat   nutrient in a wide range of foods, especially fatty ones

fatty acid   small unit that fat is broken down into during digestion

fiber   name for the parts of a carbohydrate that your body cannot break down. It is found in whole wheat foods, bran, the skin of fruits and vegetables, and beans.

fluoride   mineral often added to toothpaste to help build strong teeth

gelling agent   something that helps a food product set and gives it shape and structure

germ   part of the wheat grain. It contains some of the vitamins and fats.

glucose   smallest unit that carbohydrates can be broken down into during digestion

glycogen   name for any glucose stored in the liver and muscles following absorption. Extra glucose is stored if it is not needed immediately by the body.

hemorrhoids   collection of swollen veins around the anus caused by a diet low in fiber, which leads to straining

hormone   substance produced by different glands in the body that affect or control particular organs, cells, or tissues

ileum   third and last part of the small intestine

insoluble fiber   type of fiber that will not dissolve

jejunum   middle part of the small intestine

kilojoule   measurement of energy supplied by food

large intestine   part of the intestines through which undigested food passes after it has left the small intestine

liver   organ in the body used in the digestive system

marathon   long-distance running race

mead   fermented drink made out of honey

mineral   nutrient needed by the body in small amounts

molecule very small part of a substance

natural sugar sugar that is naturally present in food, not added

nervous system series of connected nerves throughout the body

nutrient carbohydrates, proteins, fats, vitamins, and minerals are all nutrients. Foods and most drinks contain different amounts and types of nutrients.

nutritionist person who studies nutrients and how the body uses them

obesity state of being extremely overweight

organ internal body part, such as the liver, stomach, or intestines

oxygen gas present in the air that is used by the body when we breathe in

preserve protect food from going "bad." Food can be preserved for a short time by cooking it or putting it in the refrigerator. It can be preserved for longer by freezing, canning, bottling, vacuum packing, jamming, irradiating, drying, pickling, or adding preservatives.

processed describes foods that have been changed to make them easier to prepare, cook, or eat

protein nutrient supplied by foods such as meat, fish, and nuts

small intestine part of the intestine into which food passes from the stomach to be digested and then absorbed into the bloodstream. Undigested food passes through the small intestine into the large intestine.

soluble fiber fiber that can be dissolved

villi tiny bumps in the intestines through which digested food and water is absorbed

vitamin nutrient needed by the body in small amounts

whole wheat food that uses the whole of the wheat grain

Find Out More

Books

Ballard, Carol. *Making Healthy Food Choices: Special Diets and Food Allergies.*
    Chicago: Heinemann Library, 2007.
Parker, Steve. *Our Bodies: Digestion.* Chicago: Raintree, 2004.

Websites

www.cnpp.usda.gov
This site from the Center for Nutrition Policy and Promotion, a part of the U.S. Department of Agriculture, provides information about health and nutrition. Included is the "MyPyramid" food pyramid, which offers guidelines for a healthy, balanced diet.

www.celiac.org
Find out more information about celiac disease.

www.diabetes.org
Find out more information about diabetes.

www.wheatworld.org
Learn more about wheat.

www.nationalpotatocouncil.org
Find information about potatoes.

Contacts

Center for Nutrition Policy and Promotion
3101 Park Center Drive, 10th floor
Alexandria, Virginia 22302
Tel: (703) 305-7600

American Diabetes Association
1701 North Beauregard Street
Alexandria, Virginia 22311
Tel: 1-800-DIABETES

Celiac Disease Foundation
13251 Ventura Boulevard #1
Studio City, California 91604
Tel: (818) 990-2354

Index